Augustus Louis Chetlain

The Red River Colony

Augustus Louis Chetlain

The Red River Colony

ISBN/EAN: 9783742813534

Manufactured in Europe, USA, Canada, Australia, Japa

Cover: Foto ©ninafisch / pixelio.de

Manufactured and distributed by brebook publishing software
(www.brebook.com)

Augustus Louis Chetlain

The Red River Colony

THE

Red River Colony

BY

Augustus L. Chetlain.

CHICAGO, ILL.:

1893.

PRESS OF
ROGERSON & STOCKTON
CHICAGO

I hear the tread of pioneers,
   Of nations yet to be,
The first low wash of waves where soon
   Shall roll a human sea.

                    —*Whittier*.

PREFACE.

In 1878 I wrote a sketch of the Red River colony, which was published in the December number of *Harper's Monthly Magazine* of that year. I had with difficulty obtained the facts given, as nothing written or printed could be found relating to the events that occurred at the Red River settlement between 1816 and 1830. I had to rely on such facts as could be gathered from living members of the colony. I was indebted to my mother, (who died in 1887 at the age of 88 years), whose memory was clear and correct for most of the facts directly connected with the colony given in the following sketch, which is substantially the same as that published by the Harpers. I have added a portion of the Earl of Selkirk's statement, prepared by him after his return to England from the settlement in 1816, and published in London in 1818. That the reader may have a correct idea of the unfortunate condition of affairs in the settlement from 1811 to 1816, this interesting little history is put in this form to be placed in the hands of the descendants of that brave band of emigrants, that they may not in the future be ignorant of the hardships their ancestors endured when voyaging from the fertile valleys and vine-clad slopes of the Jura to seek new homes on the inhospitable plains of the far-off Rupert Land.

A. L. CHETLAIN.

Chicago, Ills., April, 1893.

MAP OF HUDSON BAY AND THE TERRITORY WESTWARD.

The exhaustion of material forces by the
Napoleonic wars, which at their close at Water-
loo had enfeebled almost to the last gasp all
the powers that had been engaged in them,
had effects equally powerful upon the social
conditions of Europe. In this last phase,
indeed, the most deplorable results are seen.
The populations which had been reduced by
losses in battle and by disease were disheart-
ened, disorganized, impoverished. Successful
business enterprises, public and private, which
alone can restore confidence and happiness in
such a conjuncture, were impossible and unat-
tempted. Manufacturing industries at first lan-
guished, then ceased to exist. To crown all
these miseries, the untimely and excessive rains
in the summer of 1816 had so damaged the
crops that a general famine was apprehended.
The expense and difficulty of transportation

enhanced the cost of all necessaries of life. The price of grain rose to an unprecedented height, and the poorer classes suffered for the want of bread. In Switzerland the distress was greater than in any other part of Central Europe, and the people, wearied of struggles which resulted in their own impoverishment, listened eagerly to the story of a peaceful and more prosperous country beyond the sea.

A few years earlier, Thomas Dundas, Earl of Selkirk, a distinguished Scotch nobleman of great wealth, had purchased from the Hudson Bay Company a large tract of land in British America, extending from the Lake of the Woods and the Winnipeg River westward for nearly 200 miles, and from Lakes Winnipeg and Manitoba to the United States boundary, part of which tract is now embraced in the province of Manitoba, and in which are the fertile lands bordering on the Red and Assiniboine rivers. It formed a part of "Rupert Land," named in honor of Prince Rupert, or Robert, of Bavaria, a cousin of King Charles II. of England, and one of the founders and chief managers of the Hudson Bay Company. Rupert Land was somewhat indefinite in extent, embracing all that portion of British America that poured its waters into Hudson Bay, and was drained chiefly by the

Great Whale, Rupert, Abbitibbe, Albany, Severn, Winnipeg, Red, Assiniboine, Saskatchewan and Churchill rivers. In extent it was almost equal to the United States prior to its accessions after the close of the Mexican war. It was the original purpose of Lord Selkirk to settle these lands with colonists from Scotland. In the year 1811 he had succeeded in planting a large colony of Presbyterians from the north of Scotland and a few from the north of Ireland on the Red River, near its junction with the Assiniboine. This was followed, four years later, by two more, but smaller colonies from the same section of Scotland. In consequence of the stubborn competition and the bitter dissensions between the Hudson Bay Company and the Northwest Company of Montreal, these colonists were compelled to abandon their new homes, nearly all of them removing to Lower Canada, where they believed they could live in greater peace and security.

Lord Selkirk entertained great admiration for the character of the Swiss, and having failed in his emigration schemes with his own countrymen, turned his attention to Switzerland. He prepared and caused to be published in the French and German languages a pamphlet giving a full but somewhat exaggerated description of the new country, its climate, soil and productions, and offered to all heads of families, or those who were unmarried and over twenty-one years of age, land free of cost, with seeds, cattle and farming implements, all on a credit of three years. It was the policy of the British government to favor these emigration schemes, the statesmen of that day believing that the region in question could successfully be colonized and settled by way of the north route, viz: Hudson Bay, Nelson River and Lake Winnipeg. The pamphlet alluded to was freely distributed by Lord Selkirk's agents in the French-speaking cantons of Neuchatel, Vaud and Geneva, and in the German-speaking canton of Berne. Many young and middle-aged men in those cantons, having become weary of the condition of affairs at home, decided to emigrate to British America under the auspices of Lord Selkirk, and formed a colony for that purpose. It was agreed to set out for America in the spring of 1821. The colony numbered over 200 persons, nearly three-fourths of whom were of French origin and speaking that language. They were Protestants in faith, and belonged to the Reformed Lutheran Church. Many of the families were descendants of the Huguenots of Eastern France ; all were healthy, robust and well fitted

for the labor and privations incident to a life
in a new country ; most of them were liberally
educated and possessed of considerable means,
Among the more prominent heads of families
were Monnier and Rindesbacher (the senior, of
the colony in age, and men of culture and of
influence in their respective localities), Dr.
Ostertag, Chetlain (originally Chatelain) and
Descombes ; and of the unmarried, Schirmer
(afterward, for a score of years, the leading
jeweler at Galena, Illinois), Quinche and Langet. To the foregoing names might be added
those of Ehrler, Schadiker, Hombert, Tissot,
Ebersol, Sunier, Marchand, Terret, Hoffmann,
Tubac, Gilbert, Cush, Racine and Simon, most
of whom were married. In the families there
were, as it happened, but few children under
twelve years of age, except infants in arms.

In the month of May, 1821, the prelimi-
naries having been completed, the colonists
assembled at a small village on the Rhine near
Basle. Why they did not rendezvous at Basle—
a city of considerable commercial importance—
seems a little strange. The impression afterward prevailed among the colonists that the
managers feared to take them to a large city
lest some unfavorable facts connected with
the country to which they were going might
come to light, especially the important circum-

stance that Lord Selkirk had failed to settle the country with his own countrymen. Be this as it may, two large flat-boats or barges were provided for their use at the rendezvous, and in these they floated down the Rhine, with its numerous cities and villages and its vine-clad hills and ruined castles on either hand. But with hearts elated with hope, and their imaginations filled with visions of a distant land, it may be doubted if the storied scenes of that beautiful river received from these hardy adventurers more than a passing thought. At the end of ten days they reached a small village near Rotterdam, where a staunch ship, the "Lord Nelson," was in readiness to take them to the New World.

After setting sail their course lay north of Great Britain, and just south of Greenland, to Hudson Strait. Soon after their departure from Holland it was found that the quality of the food issued was greatly inferior to that promised them before their departure from Switzerland, and complaint was made to the captain of the ship—a stern, but kind-hearted old seaman, who acknowledged the wrong, but claimed that he was not responsible for it, which was no doubt true. The water also was bad, and issued in insufficient quantities. Arriving at Hudson Strait, latitude 62° north,

the Lord Nelson overtook two English ships
bound for Fort York, or York Factory, situated at the mouth of the Nelson River, laden
with Indian goods and supplies for the garri-
sons at Forts York and Douglas, and for the
employes of the Hudson Bay Company. The
strait was filled with floes and bergs of ice,
and the ships were thereby detained over
three weeks. One of the supply ships was
seriously damaged, and nearly lost, by col-
lision with an iceberg. Finally, with much
difficulty and no little peril, Hudson Bay was
entered, and after a long and tedious voyage
of nearly four months, they landed at Fort
York. The colonists were at once embarked
in bateaux, and commenced the ascent of the
Nelson River. Propelling their heavy-laden
boats by rowing, often against a strong current, at the end of twenty days Lake Winnipeg was reached, and here new troubles
awaited them. The season was advanced,
the fall storms had set in, and their progress
along the east shore of the lake, 260 miles
in length, was slow and laborious. After a
day's hard rowing, often against head-winds,
the little fleet of boats would put into some
sheltered spot, where the weary voyageurs,
perhaps drenched with rain or benumbed with
cold, would kindle fires, and all be made as

comfortable as possible for the night. In addition to these discouragements and discomforts, their supply of provisions gave out, and the few fish they were able to catch were barely sufficient to keep them from starving. At the end of three weeks, much time having been lost by reason of high winds and storms, they arrived, half famished, at the mouth of the Red River, where, to their dismay, they learned that the locusts or grasshoppers had passed through the country the summer before, literally destroying all the crops. With heavy hearts they proceeded up the river some thirty-five miles to Fort Douglas, situated on the west bank of the river, where now stands the city of Winnipeg. Governor Alexander McDonell and the other officers of the Hudson Bay Company, by their cordial welcome and earnest efforts to supply their wants and make them comfortable, not only gladdened their hearts, but did much to make them forget the hardships of their long voyage.

It is worthy of note, in passing, that three years before their arrival the Hudson Bay Company and the Northwest Company had settled their long-standing difficulties amicably, and merged their interests in a new corporation, retaining the name of the former company. Governor McDonell could not promise the colonists sufficient provisions to carry them through the approaching winter, for it was evident that the supplies received from England would be inadequate for the wants of all. After a full deliberation upon a question scarcely less momentous than that of life or death, it was resolved to send some seventy-five of the younger and more hardy of the colonists to Pembina, up the river, near the United States boundary, sixty miles distant, where it was believed the buffalo, elk and deer were more abundant, and where jerked buffalo meat and pemmican could be obtained from the Indians of that locality. Just as the winter closed in, the party arrived at Pembina, and at once set about repairing the buildings of the deserted trading post, constructing huts and procuring fuel for the winter.

The succeeding winter was long and intensely cold, the thermometer often falling to forty-five degrees below zero, and the snow unusually deep. The colonists wintering at Pembina fared badly enough. With the advance of winter, the scanty supply of provisions brought from Fort Douglas diminished rapidly, and, when exhausted, the fish, obtained with difficulty from the river through holes cut in the ice, with what buffalo meat could be bought from the Indians, was scarcely sufficient to prevent starvation. Sometimes an Indian dog was killed and eaten, and relished by most of them. The parties who occasionally ventured out with dogs and sledges, obtained from the Indians to hunt for the buffalo, met with indifferent success, owing to the scarcity of the animals that winter, and lack of experience. Several of them were maimed for life by the freezing of their hands and feet. In the spring, after the snow had disappeared, the women would gather acorns and the seed-balls of the wild-rose bush that grew rank on the margin of the river, which, when cooked with a little buffalo fat, made nutritious if not palatable food, and served to relieve the hardship and monotony of the almost exclusively fish diet of the preceding winter.

Five years prior to the advent of the Swiss colony the employes of the Northwest Company, in their bitter opposition to Lord Selkirk's scheme to colonize that country with Europeans, openly resisted the settlers, and went so far as to make an armed attack on a settlement of Scotchmen near Fort Douglas, killing some twenty of them, including Governor Robert Semple, who had received his appointment as Governor of Hudson Bay Company five years previous. Lord Selkirk, on learning of the massacre, left England at once for Canada. There he obtained from the authorities a hundred or more soldiers from the "De Meuron Regiment"* and a few volunteers. Placing himself at their head, he proceeded to the Red River Settlement, where, after seizing several of their trading-posts, he restored peace and tranquility.† Two years after, the troops brought from Canada were discharged, and the greater part of them were induced by Lord Selkirk to settle in that country. Land was donated them near Fort Douglas, and cattle and other supplies furnished them on a long credit. Fortune favored these settlers, and at the time of the arrival of the Swiss colony they were generally well-to-do farmers; and had it not been for the ravages of the grasshoppers the summer before, the crops of these farmers would have furnished ample food for the new-comers during

*Count De Meuron, a French Swiss of Neuchatel, raised a regiment of infantry, mostly in Switzerland, which was employed by the British government for operations in lower Canada, with the agreement that the men, at the end of their term of enlistment, should be given lands in any portion of Canada, free of charge.

† Mr. Henry Bradshaw Fearon published at London, in 1818, "A narrative of a journey through the Eastern and Western parts of America, together with remarks on Birbeck's Notes and Letters," (referring to the Edwards Co., Ill., settlement).

In a history of the English settlement in Edwards County, Ill., published in Chicago, in 1882, the Hon. E. B. Washburne, ex-Secretary of State, ex-Embassador and Minister Plenipotentiary to France, etc., says:

"Curiously enough, Mr. Fearon speaks of meeting, at Gwathway's Hotel, in Louisville, Ky., Lord Selkirk, who was on his 'return their first year's stay. These Canadian settlers, or "meurons," as they were called, were all unmarried, except a few who had taken Indian or half-breed wives. Among the colonists were several families in which were marriageable daughters, and it was natural that offers of marriage should be made by the bachelor farmers. During the winter several such marriages were consummated. The colonists, although disappointed and almost starving, were nevertheless cheerful, and disposed to make the most of the unfortunate circumstances in which they found themselves. It was deemed necessary to celebrate the nuptials in a becoming manner, and to do honor to the occasion a party would be given, to which the relatives and friends were bidden. Wedding cake was made of coarse flour obtained from wheat ground in the ordinary rotary coffee-mill, to which was added a little buffalo fat and salt.

from his successful expedition in the Northwest Territory.' He says he obtained for his lordship some Boston papers which were only two months old, which afforded him great satisfaction, as he had not heard any intelligence from Europe for nine months.

"This is an interesting fact, for it shows that Lord Selkirk, on leaving the settlement he had founded on the Red River of the North, did not return home by sea from York Factory or by Montreal, but made his way by land to Fort St. Anthony afterward Fort Snelling —and thence down the Mississippi River to St. Louis. Lord Selkirk formed his first colony in 1811, which was re inforced by an immigration in 1815. This colony was under the protection of the Hudson Bay and the Northwest Companies.

"The latter company undertook to expel Selkirk's colonists. When Lord Selkirk, who was then in England, heard of this, he procured

There was also the music of the violin, and the feet of the dancers kept time to the airs of Switzerland.

The health of all the colonists that winter was good, despite the severity of the winter and the insufficiency of food. The opening of spring found them ready to enter on the lands allotted them at "La Fourche," at the junction of the Red and Assiniboine rivers, and soon after the first of May the entire colony was again united. Lord Selkirk had died at Pau, France, the autumn before their departure from Switzerland, but the fact had been withheld from them until after their arrival at Fort Douglas. Consequently no provision had been made to supply them with seeds and farming implements, as promised them before their departure from the Old World. They were therefore compelled, with few exceptions, to use the ordinary hoe and

permission from the British government to take a military force from Canada to Red River to protect his settlers. With a company of regular soldiers of the British army and a certain number of volunteers, he returned with them to Red River and drove out the representatives of the Northwest Company. After this had been accomplished, finding his colony weakened by the troubles it had gone through, he determined to return to Europe to beat up recruits for another colony. The original colonists had been mostly Scotch, but now he turned his attention to procuring protestant Swiss, mostly from the Jura. This last colony, having been organized, sailed for York Factory in 1821. But in the meantime, and without the knowledge of the colonists, before they had taken their departure, Lord Selkirk had died at Pau, in France. This was a fatal blow to the success of the colony.

spade in turning over the sod and in preparing the soil for planting and sowing the seeds obtained in limited quantities from the Canadian farmers. However, as the result of a hard summer's work, the women assisting the men, and the soil being remarkably productive, the crops raised, with what they obtained from the older settlers, carried them through the succeeding winter comfortably.

Early in the fall of 1821, a herd of cattle, mostly cows, arrived from the State of Missouri, in charge of a party of armed drovers, and were distributed in the spring of 1822 among the Swiss settlers. This distribution of cattle, which had been contracted for by Lord Selkirk before his death, was all that had been done for the colonists in fulfillment of the pledges made them before their departure from Europe. As a consequence, dissatisfaction became general, and a determination was made

"Deprived of the fostering care of the founder, and with unlooked for and terrible hardships, and in the presence of frightful sufferings, the colonists were obliged to totally abandon their enterprise.

"There was no ship to take them back by the way of the sea from York Factory; the only possible escape was to the nearest settlement in the United States. Their attention was undoubtedly directed to this means of deliverance by the fact that Lord Selkirk had taken that route, when he left the country in 1818. Many of these colonists afterward settled in the Galena lead mines and became excellent citizens, distinguished by probity and honor, industry and thrift. A son of one of the prominent colonists [the author of this sketch] has written a very interesting account of the colony of 1821."

This date should be 1816 and not 1818, as given by Mr. Washburne.

by a small part of the colonists to depart, the first practicable moment, for the United States— a country of which they had learned much since their arrival at the Red River. On the return of the drovers, in the autumn of 1821, five families begged permission to accompany them, which was granted. In the month of November the party arrived in safety at Fort St. Anthony (subsequently Fort Snelling), situated at the junction of the Mississippi and St. Peter's rivers, then in process of construction, and garrisoned by United States troops in command of Colonel Josiah Snelling of the Fifth United States Infantry. With the consent of the commanding officer, the party of emigrants remained at the fort during the succeeding winter. The next spring they settled on the military reservation near the fort, cultivated land, and sold the products to the garrison.

In the spring of 1823 thirteen more of the colonists, with their families, decided to go to the United States, with the intention of settling in the State of Missouri, of which section of the Union they had heard glowing descriptions from the party of drovers two years before. They hired some half dozen carts— all that could be obtained in the settlement— to carry their effects to the head waters of the St. Peter's (now the Minnesota) River at

Lake Traverse, some 200 miles above Fort St. Anthony, by the course of the river. These carts were constructed without iron; the tires being of rawhide drawn tightly around the wheel. They are still known as the Red River cart, and, until the opening of the North Pacific railroad, were frequently seen at St. Paul. The Sioux Indians, found on their route after entering the United States, were unfriendly, if not openly hostile, and the little company were often in considerable peril. By judicious management, however, understanding as they well did the character of the Indian, they escaped open conflict. The chiefs, of the roving bands encountered, were generally appeased, and their apparent good-will gained by presents of ammunition, food and trinkets. Before the end of their journey, however, the Indians succeeded in stealing a part of their cooking utensils and provisions. The inadequate number of carts, heavily laden as they were with their effects, prevented any, except the older, children from riding, and often a mother would walk twenty miles in a day with a babe in her arms. The men were all armed, and acted as an escort to the train. After a long, and at times perilous, journey of 400 miles, they reached Lake Traverse and went into camp; the carts returning with the men to whom they belonged.

Preparations were at once begun to descend the St. Peter's river. Cottonwood trees were felled, and canoes or "dug-outs" were made; one for every two adults of the party. The work was slow and difficult for the want of proper tools. Being in a country through which roamed hunting parties of unfriendly and thieving Indians, it was neccessary to keep a guard over the camp at night. That duty devolved on the women, for the men needed the sleep of night in order to be able to work by day on the canoes. An old lady,* now in her seventy-ninth year, and the only surviving member of the colony, who was twenty years of age or more at the time of the departure of the colony from Switzerland, told the writer not long since, with evident pride, that she had more than once stood guard over that little camp, armed with a gun, from nine o'clock at night until sunrise the next morning. The canoes having been finished, the party launched them, and heading them down the stream, floated with the current the greater part of the time. The river, as is usual at that season of the year, was low, and some portions of it filled with shoals and sand-bars, over which they were often compelled to drag their heavy-laden crafts. About the middle of the

---

* Mrs. Louis Chetlain, who died Oct., 1887, at Galena.

23

month of September they arrived at Fort St.
Anthony, and were kindly received by the
officers of the garrison, and warmly welcomed
by their countrymen who had preceded them
one year before.   After a few weeks' rest they
prepared to descend the Mississippi river to
St. Louis, their destination.   Two small barges
or keel boats, which had been used to transport supplies from St. Louis for the use of the
troops, were generously placed at their disposal
by Colonel Snelling (who also supplied them
with provisions for the voyage), and in these
they leisurely floated down the river, meeting
with little or no difficulty.   The exposure and
hardships of the summer and early fall brought
on chills and fevers and other malarial diseases.
Mr. Monnier, the senior of the party in age,
fell sick and died, and was buried near Prairie
du Chien; and soon after his eldest daughter
followed him.   Before reaching Rock Island,
Mr. Chetlain became delirious with fever, and
it was decided to leave him, with his wife and
child, at Fort Amstrong, where he was placed
in the post hospital and cared for with kind-
ness and skill by Dr. Craig, the post surgeon.
The rest proceeded on their way, reaching St.
Louis late in the month of November.   Mr.
Chetlain and family joined them the next
spring.

On the arrival of the emigrants at St. Louis, then a city of 6,000 inhabitants, they were welcomed and hospitably treated by the Chouteaus, Soulards and Gratiots (the latter of Franco-Swiss origin), and other French-speaking citizens, who had become familiar with their peculiar history. The greater part of the emigrants leased lands near the city and cultivated them. They proved industrious, temperate and thrifty citizens. The climate of that region, however, was evidently unfavorable for them, and a larger part fell sick. The process of acclimation was slow and difficult, and by the end of the second summer most of them decided to remove to a cooler and more healthful climate. The opening of the lead mines of the Northwest gave the wished-for opportunity. Mr. Chetlain and a few others, with their families, joined Colonel Henry Gratiot, the newly appointed United States agent for the Winnebago Indians, and took passage on the steamboat Mexico — one of the first boats that ascended the Mississippi above the mouth of the Illinois River — for La Pointe, on Fever River, where now stands the city of Galena; arriving there the 14th day of April, 1826. Some months later, Messrs. Schirmer, Langet and others followed. In the autumn of that year the greater part of them removed to the Indian agency at Gratiot's Grove, fifteen miles northeast from La Pointe, and engaged in mining and smelting lead ore, and in farming.

The spring of 1826 was noted for the great rise of water in the Mississippi and its tributaries, and in the Red and Assiniboine rivers, caused by the unusual deep snow of the preceding winter, which had melted with warm and heavy rains. The Red and Assiniboine rivers rose so high that the lands at La Fourche were completely inundated, and the settlers compelled to seek safety by flight to higher ground, several miles distant, taking with them their cattle and household effects. The losses, sustained by the flood, were very great, and no efforts were made to repair them. Nearly all the Swiss settlers remaining at La Fourche, including a part of the Canadian settlers, having become thoroughly discouraged, decided to leave at once for the United States. Abandoning their lands, and selling their cattle and farming implements for what they could, they hired carts to transport their effects and provisions, and started in a body for Fort St. Anthony, following the route taken by the first party (three years before) to Lake Traverse, and from thence by land to their destination, arriving there early in the autumn of that year. Governor McDonell and the other officers of the Hudson Bay Company deeply regretted their departure, and generously supplied them with provisions for the journey free of cost, an interpreter, a guide, and an armed escort of forty-five men. A few weeks after their arrival at Fort St. Anthony they were fortunate enough to find a small steamboat that had been used to transport supplies for the troops at that point, in which they took passage for the lead mines, to which place they decided to go after they had reached Fort St. Anthony. On their arrival at La Pointe they were warmly welcomed by their countrymen who had preceded them. Some of them settled at La Pointe, while the greater part went out to the agency at Gratiot's Grove and engaged in mining and farming.

Six years later, when the Indian troubles began which culminated in a war known as the "Black Hawk War," and volunteers were called for, nearly all the men, without regard to age, enlisted, and, having been accustomed to the use of firearms, rendered the country of their adoption valuable service.

The descendants of these colonists are numerous, and are found scattered throughout the Northwest, the greater part being in the region of the lead mines. Most of them are thrifty farmers and stockbreeders. A few have

entered the professions and trade. All, as far
as is known, are temperate, industrious and
law-abiding citizens.

LETTER FROM MRS. GRISARD (*née* SIMON).

GEN. A. L. CHETLAIN.

Dear Sir and Friend: I can offer no excuse for not acknowledging your kind letter and the *Harper* of 1878, except the desire to write you with my own hand. The description in the *Harper* was entirely correct, and, if I were with you and your dear mother, we would, without doubt, in talking over that terrible voyage, recollect many things. The ship that was run into by the iceberg was the "Lord Nelson." We were three ships fastened to the iceberg, and at one time there were five — two exploring vessels laden with merchandise for Quebec, and the two others for Ft. York. Mme. Quinche (*née* Monnier,) must remember that when we were invited on to one of the other ships, that, in returning, she fell into the water, greatly to our fright. On our voyage we were so near the North

Pole that it was continually day — there being only from fifteen to twenty minutes that we could not see to read on deck. Captain May, the Secretary of Lord Selkirk, had assured me that the climate on the borders of the Red River was perfect, maturing all kinds of grain and fruits; so the visits of the Esquimaux to our ship was another surprise, and showed us what high latitude we were in. Arriving at Ft. York, there were not enough boats for transporting our baggage, so we were obliged to leave everything that was not absolutely necessary for the winter, with the promise that in the spring everything would be delivered in good order at Ft. Douglass, on Red River; but I do not know if the things ever arrived, for we left the colony the spring of 1822, after the second devastation from "grasshoppers," which covered the earth, coming like a great thunderstorm. As you say, we distributed ourselves among the Meurons, who belonged to a regiment commanded by a Swiss, of Neuchatel — Count de Meuron — who, much to our disappointment, was absent during our stay there. I do not remember his name, but his parents were sugar-refiners in Neuchatel at that time. During our stay there our expenses were great. Wheat was two dollars a bushel, and was ground in our own coffee-mills (mine we still keep as a relic); potatoes were the same price, but meat was only twelve pounds for one dollar; coffee, two dollars a pound; the same with tobacco; sugar, one dollar a pound, and salt, one dollar a quart. Our suffering was great toward spring, when there was a lack of all provisions, at which time we lived on fish, without even salt. Sturgeon and cat-fish are very large in that river. From that time my father decided to leave the colony. He chartered two boats, with two hunters to row and provide us with game. Arrived at Pembina, which at that time was considered to be in the English territory, we found the Sioux Indians on the war-path, which made traveling by water too dangerous, so we hired two carts, with guides, who drove cattle for Lord Selkirk, and with the two hunters for protection we went from Pembina to the River St. Peter (now Minnesota). Mamma and myself were the first white women who had ever crossed those prairies, and the danger was terrible. When leaving Pembina, all the half-breeds and Canadians said it would not be three days before the Indians would be danc-ing with the scalps of those white women, but God protected us, though many times I came near being captured, but our guides were faith-ful and on the alert; but, what is strange, those very same Indians recognized me at Fort Snelling, and told the interpreters how they had laid their plans to capture me. At Lake Traverse we were obliged to stop quite a time, as it was just the time that the Indians were there to receive their annuities from the government. At that time we heard that you had crossed without being massacred, and a number of families joined us there (among which were the Quinches), where we were cutting the trees to make our canoes, and as we had dismissed the hunters we only had the guides and my father, who was not accustomed to work, so the other families made their canoes long before us, and before we left the place we almost died of hunger. For two whole days we had not one mouthful to eat; on the third we met some Indians who were picking wild rice. They took us to their tents and fed us bountifully with soup and little pieces of meat that were cooking on the fire when we came. We stayed with them two days.

Your list of names was correct, but I think I remember a family of Junot, and one named Jacard.

Arriving at Fort Snelling, I was received like a sister by Mme. Colonel Snelling, in whose family I stayed while there. Each day my father came and gave French lessons to Miss and Mrs. Snelling, and so our stay was lucrative as well as agreeable.

In the spring of 1823 a steamboat arrived there, named the "Virginia." This was the first steamboat that had ascended the Mississippi above the mouth of the Illinois River. It had been three weeks coming from St. Louis, as it did not run nights. The winter of 1822-23 was a remarkable one. During a number of weeks the garrison of Fort St. Peter was on the alert, fearing a surprise from the Indians, who were then massed together so near the fort that the sound of their war-cry was heard. Their plan was to massacre the whole garrison. From that time no Indian was allowed to come into the fort.

My father was a teacher, and did not have enough occupation, so we left for St. Louis, arriving in good health. We were introduced into the families of Soulards and Chouteaus. Mrs. James G. Soulard and Colonel Snelling were brother and sister. Our stay there was pleasant, and my father had plenty of lucrative work (there being only one young lady who gave French lessons, a Miss Favre); but it was unhealthy at St. Louis, and my father wished to come here, where the settlers were almost entirely Vaudois Suisse. He died five weeks after our arrival.

I continued, for some time, to keep a little school, but at last had to turn my attention to the sewing for the family. I was accustomed to fancy sewing, but at that time the necessaries of life were all one could possibly perform.

In 1825 I married Fred G. Grisard, from Villeret, Canton of Berne. We lived happily until January 30th, 1881, when he died.

Each day grows sadder, though I have my eldest daughter with me, and my children are all kind, and I have abundantly of this world's goods. I thank God, hoping that some day not distant I shall join my husband, for I am past seventy-seven years.

Accept my assurance of esteem, and, if you ever come to Vevay, I shall be delighted to have a visit from you.

Very truly,

ZELIE C. GRISARD,

nee Zelie C. Simon.

Vevay, Indiana, December 21st, 1884.

DAVID MONNIER.—Born in the Canton of Neuchatel. He was a man of education, probity of character, and of kind disposition. He had a large family—six daughters and two sons. His daughters married Quinche, Shirmer, the Jaccards and Estey, all of whom are dead. His son, a farmer and stockbreeder, died not long since near Galena, leaving a large family. Mr. Monnier and his eldest daughter died in 1823 while descending the Mississippi River from Fort St. Anthony to St. Louis. His grandchildren are quite numerous, and are living in Galena and vicinity, and in St. Louis. One granddaughter—the daughter of the late Augustus Estey, a banker in Galena, and wife of Capt. W. A. Montgomery, a prominent lawyer—is living in Chicago.

PETER RINDESBACHER.—A native of the Canton of Berne, senior of the colonists, and sometimes called Father Rindesbacher; by force of character he was recognized as their leader. He died over a score of years ago on his farm in Jo Daviess County, Illinois. He had a numerous family, all of whom are now dead, except Mrs. Charles Monnier. His eldest daughter married Doctor Ostertag. Some years after the doctor's death she married Mr. Collins. The children and grandchildren are living in southwestern Wisconsin. His second son, Peter, born in Switzerland, was a young man of great promise. He early developed a taste for music and painting. When in St. Louis, he was placed in a studio of a portrait painter of some note. He had some creditable sketches of Indians and of wild animals—done in a somewhat crude way at the Red River settlement—that attracted the attention of some United States army officers at St. Louis, who later took him with them on military excursions up the Missouri River. He excelled in portrait-painting on ivory. He died in St. Louis at the age of twenty-eight. It has been stated by competent judges of his work that, had he lived, he would have ranked as an artist with Stanly and Catlin. The third son, Frederick, an extensive farmer of Jo Daviess County, died some years ago, leaving a large family, among whom two are sons prominent citizens in that section of the country.

ALFRED QUINCHE.- Married the second daughter of Mr. Monnier, and had numerous children. Two of his sons are now living in Kansas. Alfred, the second son, who died some years since, was extensively engaged for many years in mining and smelting lead ore near Shullsburg, Wisconsin. The fourth son, Alexander, received a collegiate education and took a theological course preparatory to entering the ministry. Soon after entering the ministry, he accepted the chair of Literature in the Oxford University of the State of Mississippi. He ranked high in his profession, and died some years ago after twenty-eight years' continuous service in that institution. He left a widow and two daughters, now living.

PHILIP F. SHIRMER.—A man of rare intelligence, great energy, good business qualifications and strong religious convictions, was born at Geneva. He married Miss Monnier. There were born to them five children. The eldest son, David, died some years ago; Philip is a merchant in St. Louis; Mrs. Barker, widow of the late Dr. W. S. Barker, a prominent physician of St. Louis; Mrs. Catlin (widow) and Miss Henrietta, are living in St.

Louis, and Mrs. Miller (widow), in Denver, Colorado.

LOUIS CHETLAIN (originally Chatelain).—Of Tramelan, Canton of Berne, Switzerland, married Julie Hombert Droz, of Ligneres, Canton of Neuchatel, in 1820. There were born to them eleven children, five of whom are now living: Frederick, the eldest son, one of the best known and most highly-esteemed men in the lead mine region, and the manager of the Chetlain farm, near Galena, after the death of his father, in 1873, died over a year ago. Of Augustus, the second son, Appleton's Encyclopædia of American Biography says:

"AUGUSTUS LOUIS CHETLAIN.—Born in St. Louis, Missouri, December 26th, 1824. His parents, of French Huguenot stock, emigrated from Neufchatel, Switzerland, in 1821, and were members of the Red River colony. He received a common school education, became a merchant in Galena, and was the first volunteer at a meeting, held in response to the President's call, after the bombardment of Fort Sumpter, in 1861. He was chosen captain of the company when General (then captain) U. S. Grant declined, and on May 1st, 1861, was commissioned lieutenant-colonel of the Twelfth Illinois infantry. He was in command at Smithland, Kentucky, from September, 1861,

till January, 1862, and then participated in
Gen. C. F. Smith's campaign on the Tennessee
River to Fort Henry, and led his regiment at
Fort Donaldson. He was engaged at Shiloh,
distinguishing himself at Corinth, being left in
command of that post until May, 1863, and
while there superintended the organization of
the first colored regiment raised in the West.
On December 13th, 1863, he was promoted
brigadier-general, placed in charge of the organization of colored troops in Tennessee, and
afterward in Kentucky, and by January 1st,
1864, had raised a force of 17,000 men, for
which service he was brevetted major-general.
From January to October, 1865, he commanded
the post and forces of Memphis, and then the
district of Talladega, Alabama, until February
5th, 1866, when he was mustered out of service.
He was assessor of internal revenue for the district of Utah and Northern Wyoming in 1867-9,
then U. S. Consul at Brussels, and after his
return to the United States in 1872, established
himself in Chicago as a banker and stockbroker.
In 1872 he organized the Home National Bank
of Chicago, and became its president. In September, 1886, General Chetlain delivered the
annual address before the Society of the Army
of the Tennessee, at Rock Island, Ill. In 1891
he organized the Industrial Bank of Chicago,

and was elected president of its board of directors." He has one son, Arthur H. Chetlain, a lawyer, now First Assistant Corporation Counsel of Chicago.

Henry, the youngest son of Louis Chetain, is now in charge of the Chetlain farm. Charles Edward, a merchant, died in 1873. The daughters living are Mrs. Capt. T. G. Drening and Mrs. D. N. Corwith, of Galena, and Mrs. T. H. Davis, of Grundy Center, Iowa.

FRANCOIS LONGETTE (originally Langet).— A farmer of West Galena, died many years ago, leaving two children—Charles, still living on the old farm, and Mrs. Calderwood, of Galena.

DESCOMBS.—The Descombs located in Missouri, near St. Louis. A number of their children and grandchildren are now living in Missouri and California.

SCHADIKER.—Mr. and Mrs. Schadiker were people of more than ordinary culture. They left the settlement at an early date and took up their residence at Fort St. Anthony.* The daughter married Sergeant Adams, afterwards Captain Adams of U. S. A. Captain Adams, as an officer, was appreciated for his many

---

* Mrs. Gen. Van Cleve, in her work, "Three Score Years and Ten: Life-long Memories of Fort Snelling, Minnesota," alludes to the Schadikers and other members of the colony who stopped at Fort St. Anthony on their way to St. Louis and Galena.

soldierly qualities. He died some years ago, leaving a widow, who now is living in Evanston, Illinois.

The children and grandchildren of Varing, Erhler, Brickler, Gerber, Tachio and Switzer are living in the lead mine region.

LOUIS CHETLAIN.   PHILIP L. SHIRMER.
              PETER RINDESBACHER.
PROF. ALEXANDER QUINCHE.   GEN. A. L. CHETLAIN.

APPENDIX.

STATEMENT, ETC., OF THE EARL OF SELKIRK.

The plans of colonization, promoted by the Earl of Selkirk in British North America, have, for some time past, given rise to much, and gross, misrepresentation. More than common pains have been taken, by his opponents, to mislead, and prejudice, the public:—but such attempts, when the opportunity for strict investigation arrives, can have no other effect than to recoil upon those whose studied object has been to calumniate an individual, and conceal the truth. It is therefore extremely desirable that the real circumstances of the case should be better understood, and that the true nature, and extent of those extraordinary acts, by which his plans have hitherto been thwarted, should be developed. The documents which I have to produce, and the facts which I am enabled to state, cannot fail to throw much light upon the subject. These I shall endeavor to submit as clearly, and concisely, as possible,—but it will be requisite to trace them shortly from their commencement.

In doing so, I conceive, it will not be necessary for me to enter upon the general subject of the emigration from this country to North America ; or the views of the Earl of Selkirk in forming that settlement which has been the

47

object of such enmity and misrepresentation --His Lordship's sentiments on the general question of emigration have been long before the public ; and, since he first drew its attention, in 1805, to this important subject, a marked change has taken place, not only in the opinions of many of those who then disagreed with him, but also in the conduct of Government, which has, of late years, humanely afforded every reasonable facility for the conveyance, to our own colonies, of those emigrants (chiefly from Ireland and Scotland), who were but too much disposed to settle in the United States.

The Earl of Selkirk having, in the year 1811, obtained from the Hudson's Bay Company, a grant of land within the territory bestowed upon them by their Charter, proceeded, in conformity with one of the principal objects of the conveyance, to establish agricultural settlers upon the lands he had so obtained.—The right to the soil, as vested in the Company, and the legality of the grant, were fully supported by the opinions of several of the most eminent counsel in England,—of Sir Samuel Romilly, Mr. (now Mr. Justice) Holroyd, Mr. Cruise, Mr. Scarlett, and Mr. Bell.—His Lordship therefore proceeded, without delay, to make the requisite arrangements for the proposed settlement. —The Hudson's Bay Company, as empowered by their Charter, appointed Mr. Miles Macdonell, formerly Captain of the Queen's Rangers, to be Governor of the district of Ossiniboia, within which the settlement was to be formed, and the same gentleman was nominated, by the Earl of Selkirk, to superintend the colony, and take charge of the settlers.

In the autumn of the following year, (1812), Mr. Miles Macdonell, with a small party, arrived at the spot which had been selected for the settlement. --He immediately proceeded to erect houses, and make every necessary preparation for the arrival of the first detatchment of settlers, which was soon expected. The situation which had been chosen for the colony was on the banks of the Red River, (lat. 5c° North, long. 97° West of London,) about forty or fifty miles from its entrance into Lake Winipic, and near its confluence with the Ossiniboyne River.—At the beginning of the year 1813, the settlement consisted of about an hundred persons.—In June, 1814, they received an addition of fifty more, and in September following, the total number of settlers, and labourers, amounted to about two hundred.—In the course of the same year, between eighty and ninety additional emigrants, from the Highlands of Scotland, arrived at Hudson's Bay, for the purpose of proceeding to the settlement, having been induced to join their friends and relations at Red River, from the favourable accounts'which the latter had transmitted to them, of the lands upon which they were settling, and the flattering prospects that awaited them.—This last mentioned party, however, did not arrive at the settlement until after it was broken up, for the first time, as shall be noticed in the sequel.

From the commencement of the Red River settlement until the winter of 1814-15, and the following spring, there occurred nothing of any material importance to interrupt the progress of this infant colony*.—The difficulties, which were in some degree unavoidable at the beginning of an establishment of that nature, were happily got over.—The heads of families, as they arrived, were put in possession of regular lots of land, which they

---

* It was named the *Kildonan Settlement*, from the name of the parish, in the county of Sutherland, from whence the greater part of the settlers had emigrated.

immediately began to cultivate :—houses were built ; a mill was erected ; sheep and cattle were sent up to the settlement : and all practicable means were taken to forward the agricultural purposes of the colony. The spot which had been selected, had been ascertained to be of the highest fertility, and of the most easy cultivation. Though woods abounded in the neighbourhood, containing a variety of the finest timber, yet no trees were required to be cut down, or roots to be cleared away, from the lands that were appropriated to husbandry.—The expensive and tedious operation of clearing away heavy woods, before the ground can be tilled, (a measure indispensable in most of the new settlements in North America) was totally unnecessary upon the banks of the Red River :—the plough, from the first, met with no obstruction, and the soil proved in the highest degree rich and productive.— The climate had long been ascertained to be equal to that of any part of Canada, and with less snow in the winter.

The river abounded with fish, the extensive plains with buffaloe, and the woods with elk, deer, and game. The hunting grounds of the Indians were not at all interfered with ; and, by the term of the grant, both the grantee, and those who held under him as settlers, were entirely precluded from being concerned in the fur trade. The district indeed had almost already been exhausted of those animals, whose furs are so valuable.—The neighbouring tribes of Indians (the Sautoux) proved, from the first, to be friendly, and well-disposed.—Serious attempts indeed had been made, as early as the spring of 1813, by the clerks and interpreters employed by the fur traders from Montreal, to instigate the natives against the settlers.—The Indians were told by these persons, that it was intended to deprive them of their hunting grounds, and that. if the

establishment at the Red River once obtained a firm footing, the natives would be made slaves of by the colonists.—
These attempts to alienate the good-will of the natives
from the settlers appeared, at first, to have an alarming
effect, producing menaces, and jealousy, on the part of
their Indian neighbours.— Mr. Miles Macdonell, the Governor of the district, soon found means, however, of
doing away the unfavorable impressions which had been
raised.—He held conferences with the Sautoux tribes, and
not only succeeded in obtaining the continuance of their
friendship, but also the promise of their supreme chief to
encourage the Indians of Lake la Pluie to draw nearer
towards the Red River, for the purpose of planting Indian
corn, and establishing villages.—From this period the
Indians, in the neighbourhood, were upon the most
friendly footing with the colonists, and continued so to
the last without interruption.—There appeared, therefore,
nothing likely to occur which would impede the settlers in
their agricultural pursuits, nor were they themselves
apprehensive of any molestation.—The Earl of Selkirk, at
the commencement of the settlement, had sent up some
light brass field-pieces, swivels, and muskets, for its protection ; and an additional quantity of arms and ammunition, which had been furnished by Government for the
defence of the colony, was received there in the summer
of 1814.—In short, the settlers appeared confident of
their security, contented with their situation, and happy
in their prospects : nor did there exist any reasonable
ground to doubt, that, if left undisturbed, the colony in a
few years would have been completely, and firmly, established.—This indeed, must have been the decided opinion
at the time, even of those who proved to be its most invet-
erate opponents, otherwise they never would have thought

it necessary to take violent means to destroy it.—Had the settlement been likely to fail from causes inherent in its nature, or arising from the remoteness of its situation, or other local circumstances, its enemies (and none were better judges than they) would doubtless have left it to its fate; and, remaining passive spectators of its destruction, would gladly have permitted the colony to die a natural death, instead of incurring anxiety, expense, and the risk of the vengeance of the law, by adopting those active measures, to which they resorted, for the purpose of strangling it in its infancy.—By the enemies of this colony, I mean the North-West Company* of Fur Traders at Montreal,—whose hostility to the settlement and outrages against their fellow subjects, have been carried to a pitch so dreadful, as almost to surpass belief. It may be proper, in a few words, to trace their enmity from its commencement."

*   *   *   *   *

The foregoing statement continues at considerable length, and gives a detailed account of the outrageous conduct of the partners or directors, clerks, employees and servants of the North-West Fur Company in their efforts to destroy the settlement. Threats and intimidations were followed by the seizure of the cannons, firearms and ammunition of the settlers furnished them by the Earl of Selkirk to protect the settlement, the burning of their homes, and finally by an attack on Gover-

---

* Although the North-West Fur Traders of Montreal commonly go by the name of a *Company*, they are not a chartered body.— An account of the origin and constitution of this powerful association may be seen in a pamphlet lately published by the Earl of Selkirk, entitled, "A Sketch of the British Fur Trade in North America," etc., etc.

nor Semple and his party, which resulted in the massacre of the Governor and over twenty of his followers.

In 1816, the Earl of Selkirk, having learned that the North-West Company intended to drive out of the country the settlers, and that the work had already been begun, at once sailed from England for Canada. Here, having received more definite information of the outrages committed, he obtained from the government the services of a company of the De Meuron regiment, and also that of a number of armed volunteers. With this force he proceeded to the settlement at Red River, at first called Kildonan.

He broke up several trading posts belonging to the North-West Company and arrested a number of the leaders, who were taken to Montreal to be tried by the courts. Unfortunately, however, with few exceptions all the colonists or settlers left the country, most of them making their way to Lower Canada, a few returning to their native country by way of the Hudson Bay route. Soon after the return of the Earl to England in 1816, the Hudson Bay Company having absorbed the North-West Company, and peace having been restored, he turned his attention to the matter of securing settlers for the Red River country.

The French-Swiss colony of 1821 was the result of his efforts.

I give below one of a half score of affidavits of eye witnesses, taken by the Earl at Montreal, relating to the destruction of the settlement in 1816. Also a statement by Mr. Prichard, one of the settlers and superintendent of the colony.

Deposition of P. C. Pambrun.

Before me, Thomas Earl of Selkirk, one of his
Majesty's justices, assigned to keep the peace in the
western district of Upper Canada, appeared. Pierre
Chrisologue Pambrun, who, being duly sworn on the
Holy Evangelists, deposes, that in the month of April
last, he was sent to the trading post of the Hudson's
Bay Company, at *Qui Appelle*, by order of the deceased
Governor Semple, from whom the deponent received a
letter of instruction, a copy of which he has attested as
relation hereto.—That when he arrived, he found that
at the fort or trading post of the North-West Company,
near the same place, were assembled, a great number of
the men, commonly called Brules, Metifs, or half-breeds,
viz. the bastard sons of Indian concubines, kept by the
partners or servants of the North-West Company ; that
these people had been collected from a great distance,
some of them having come from Cumberland House,
and others from the Upper Saskatchwan, or Fort des
Prairies; that they uttered violent threats against the
colonists on the Red River, in which the deponent
understood them to be encouraged by Mr. Alexander
M'Donell, then commanding for the North-West Com-

55

pany.—That in the beginning of May, Mr. George Sutherland, commanding the Hudson's Bay post, embarked with the deponent and twenty-two men, in five boats, loaded with twenty-two packs of furs, and about six hundred bags of pemican.—That as they were going down the river on or about the 12th day of May, they were attacked by a party of forty-nine servants of the North-West Company, composed partly of Canadians and partly of half-breeds, under the command of Cuthbert Grant, Thomas M'Kay. Roderick M'Kenzie and Peter Pangman Bostonois, clerks or interpreters of the North-West Company, and Brisbois, a guide in their service, by whom they were attacked with force of arms and taken prisoners, and brought to the fort of the North-West Company, when the deponent saw Mr. Alexander M'Donell, who avowed that it was by his order that the said Grant and others had taken them prisoners, and seized on the provisions and other property of the Hudson's Bay Company, pretending that the measure was justifiable, in retaliation for Mr. Robertson's having lately taken the North-West Company's fort at the Forks of Red River, and declaring that it was his intention to starve the colonists and servants of the Hudson's Bay Company, till he should make them surrender.—That after having retained, for five days, the servants of the Hudson's Bay Company, taken prisoners as aforesaid, the said Alexander M'Donell liberated them, after having made them promise not to take up arms against the North-West Company, but the deponent was still kept in close confinement. That towards the end of May, the said Alexander M'Donell embarked in his boats and proceeded down the river, escorted by a party of half-breeds on horseback, who followed them by land, and that he carried with him the provisions and furs which his people had taken on the 12th. That the deponent was made to embark in one of the boats, and as they were coming down the river, he was told by several of the servants of the North-West Company, that Alexander M'Donell had said the business of last year was a trifle in comparison with that which would take place this year, and that the North-West Company and the half-breeds were now one and the same. That, at the Forks of Ossiniboyne River, they met a Sautoux chief with his band, to whom the said Mr. M'Donell made a speech, the purport of which was that the English (meaning the settlers on Red River, and the servants of the Hudson's Bay Company) were spoiling the lands which belonged to the Indians and half-breeds only : that they were driving away the buffaloe, and would render the Indians poor and miserable, but that the North-West Company would drive them away since the Indians did not choose to do it : that if the settlers resisted, the ground should be drenched with their blood; that none should be spared ; that he did not need the assistance of the Indians, but nevertheless he would be glad if some of their young men would join him. —That when the party came within a few miles of the Hudson's Bay Company's fort at Brandon House, the said Cuthbert Grant was sent with a party of about twenty-five men, who took the post and pillaged it of every thing, including not only the goods, provisions, and furs, belonging to the Company, but also the private property of their servants, which the deponent saw distributed among the servants of the North-West Company, Canadians as well as half-breeds.—That after this, the said M'Donell divided his forces into brigades, and

57

Cuthbert Grant, Lacerpe, Alexander Fraser, and Antoine Hoole, were appointed to command different brigades, and that Seraphim Lamar acted as lieutenant over the whole, under the said M'Donell; that the whole force amounted to about one hundred and twenty men, among whom there were six Indians.—That on arriving at portage des Prairies, the pemican was landed, and arranged so as to form a small fort, guarded by two brass swivels, which had been taken last year from the stores of the settlement. That on or about the 18th of June, two days after their arrival at portage des Prairies, the said Grant, Lacerpe, Fraser, and Hoole, and Thomas M'Kay, were sent with about seventy men to attack the colony, and the said M'Donell, with several of his officers, and about forty men, remained with the pemican. That in the evening of the 20th of June, a messenger arrived from Cuthbert Grant, who reported that they had killed Governor Semple, with five of his officers and sixteen of his men.   *   *   *   *   *

Sworn before me, at Fort Willians, on the 16th day of August, 1816.

SELKIRK, J. P.

STATEMENT OF MR. PRICHARD.*

In the course of the winter we were much alarmed by reports that the half-breeds were assembling in all parts of the North for the purpose of driving us away, and that they were expected to arrive at the settlement early in the spring.

The nearer the spring approached the more prevalent these reports grew, and letters received from different posts confirmed the same. Our hunters and those free Canadians who had supplied us with provisions were much terrified with the dread of the punishment they might receive for the support they had given us. My neighbours, the half-breeds, began to show a disposition to violence. and threatened to shoot our hunter Bollenaud's horse, and himself, too, if he did not desist from running the buffaloe ; at the same time they told me that if I did not prevent him from so doing they would go in a body on horseback, drive the cattle away and cause my people to starve.

In the month of March, Messrs. Fraser and Hesse arrived at my neighbour's house, which gave us great

* One of the settlers and superintendent of the settlement at Red River in the winter of 1815 and 1816.

uneasiness, as Fraser 'represented as the leader of the half-breeds, and that he was a daring and violent man. On his arrival he sent a threatening message to one of my hunters, and whenever an opportunity offered he was very assiduous in his endeavors to seduce from us our servants and settlers; likewise, a report was very current that a party of half-breeds and Cree Indians were expected to arrive from Fort des Prairies, on the Saskatchawan River, as soon as the melting of the snow would admit of their traveling, and the language of every free Canadian we saw was "Luefiez vous bien pour l'amour de Dieu ; mefiez vous bien."

At the same time we were informed that the half-breeds of the North-West Company who were then in the plains were ordered home to their house. This assemblage of those men gave the most serious apprehension for the safety of the settlers and those servants who were employed to bring provisions from the plains to the fort.

www.ingramcontent.com/pod-product-compliance
Lightning Source LLC
Chambersburg PA
CBHW031748090426
42739CB00008B/932